CALIFORNIA CONDORS

A TRUE BOOK

by

Patricia A. Fink Martin

Children's Press®
A Division of Scholastic Inc.

New York Toronto London Auckland Sydney
Mexico City New Delhi Hong Kong
Danbury, Connecticut

A condor cleans its feathers before flight.

Reading Consultant
Nanci R. Vargus, Ed.D.
Primary Multiage Teacher
Decatur Township Schools,
Indianapolis, IN

Content Consultant
Kathy Carlstead, Ph.D.
Honolulu Zoo

*The photo on the cover shows
a curious California condor. The
photo on the title page shows
a condor spreading its wings.*

Library of Congress Cataloging-in-Publication Data

Martin, Patricia A. Fink
    California condors / by Patricia A. Fink Martin
        p. cm. – (A True book)
    Includes bibliographical references and index.
    Summary: Describes the physical characteristics, behavior, habitat, and
endangered status of California condors.
        ISBN 0-516-22161-2 (lib. bdg.)   0-516-27470-8 (pbk.)
    1. California condor—Juvenile literature. [1. California condor.
2. Condors. 3. Endangered species.] I. Title. II. Series.
QL696.F33 M36 2002
598.9'2—dc21
                                                                    2001032296

Contents

California condors have existed for thousands of years.

A Prehistoric Bird

The California condor has lived on Earth for thousands of years. When woolly mammoths, giant sloths, and mastodons roamed North America, the condor was there. When saber-toothed tigers hunted and killed the mammoths and other giants, the condor was there.

And when the remains were left to rot, the condor was probably there too!

Why? The condor is a **scavenger**—it eats dead flesh. It once fed on dead mammoths and mastodons. Now it eats the dead flesh of cattle and deer. The California condor belongs to a group of birds called **vultures**. You may know a relative of the condor, the turkey vulture. These big black birds circle high in the sky.

A condor is part of a group of birds called vultures.

Their bodies and wings form a V when they fly.

The condor is built for feeding on large animals and riding the winds. It stands 4 feet (1.2 meters) tall from head to tail. When it unfolds its wings, they spread 9.5 feet (2.9 m) across. A large, curved beak sticks out from the front of its head. Its long neck lets it reach far into a dead body to feed. Unlike most birds, the head and neck of the condor have no feathers. Feathers would only get covered with blood and rotting flesh. Condors clean up after they eat. They wash with sand or a splash of water.

From the neck down, the condor has a coat of mostly

Condors have very large wingspans (top). Beneath a condor's black wings is a row of white feathers (bottom).

coal black feathers. Beneath its wings you can see a row of white feathers.

Scientists have uncovered condor fossils in New York, Florida, and the western United States. But by the 1800s, the condor was seldom seen across much of the country. The large bird lived mostly along the Pacific coast. Since 1973, the condor has been listed as an **endangered species**. Today most condors live in zoos. Wild condors fly free in just a few places in California and Arizona.

This condor lives
in a cage at the
Los Angeles Zoo.

Lift Off!

The condor is North America's largest flying land bird. Watching this bird fly is an amazing sight. From the ground, it looks like a small airplane. You can hear the wind whistling through its feathers. When it flaps its wings, the sound carries for a half mile (0.8 kilometer).

Two condors soar high above the ground.

A big bird such as the condor can't fly all of the time. It must wait for special winds to form. In the early morning, the condor cleans its feathers,

13

sunbathes, or simply rests high in a tree or on a cliff.

As the condor waits, sunlight hits the ground. The air near the surface warms up. The warmed air rises upward, producing a wind or current of air. This type of air current is called a **thermal**.

From its high perch, the condor leaps into the rising air, holding its big wide wings straight out. The air current carries the bird away. To turn,

A condor will leap from its perch to catch a thermal.

the condor tilts its body or moves its tail feathers. The condor rides the thermals for hours. It hardly flaps its wings at all.

The Wings

A bird's wing is made up of the same bones that you have in your arms. And like your arms, the condor's wing can bend in three places. But your wrist and hand bones are short. The condor's long wrist and hand bones help make up its giant wings.

You can turn your arms into condor wings. All you'll need are two 12-inch (30-centimeter) rulers and masking tape. Tape the end of each ruler to each hand. Extend both arms out at your shoulders.

A condor's wings bend in three places.

How far do your pretend wings reach? Have someone measure the distance from tip to tip. Remember, however, that you're just a young condor! An adult condor's wings grow much longer.

Now tuck your elbows close to your body. Bring your wrists up close to your shoulders and bend your wrists downward. This is how a condor holds its wings when it is perched.

The Clean-Up Crew

Rising air currents can lift the California condor at least a mile (1.6 km) high. As it flies, it searches for food. The condor eats only dead animals, which can include cattle, sheep, deer, horses, and ground squirrels.

How can these scavengers see from such a height?

A condor has found
something to eat.

A condor has very sharp eyesight.

Condors have excellent eye-sight and are able to spot food from far away. They are also smart animals. As they fly, they watch **predators** such as hawks and eagles. When one drops to the ground, the condor quickly follows. Sometimes condors form search parties. Together, they search the ground. When one condor spots food, the others follow.

Several condors may feed around a dead animal. How does

A group of condors gathers around a dead animal.

the condor bite into its food? Condors don't have any teeth to tear their food apart, and their claws aren't sharp like those of an eagle. Instead, condors use their strong beaks to tear their food.

A condor eats a lot at one time, and puts the extra food in a special pouch in its throat. After digesting all that food, the condor won't be hungry again for days. The pouch is also used to carry food to its young.

The large pouch under the condor's beak is used to store food.

Raising a Family

Condors don't start a family until they are at least five years old. First they select a mate. A male condor attracts a female by dancing. With his head bent, he spreads his wings apart. Slowly he moves from side to side. If the female accepts the male, the

A female condor selects a mate.

pair stays together. After a few weeks, they mate.

Next the pair searches for a nest site. Condors build their nests on cliffs, in spaces between large rocks, and in caves. Here their egg will be safe from predators. Condors don't build nests like other birds. With their heads and feet, they scrape a small hole in the dirt. The female condor lays one light-colored egg there.

This condor laid her egg in the dirt.

For the next two months, the condor parents keep the egg warm. One **incubates** the egg by sitting on it, while the other searches for food. After two to three days, they switch. Inside the shell, a baby condor grows.

When it is ready, the baby condor breaks the shell. First it makes a hole big enough to stick its head through. The baby condor now gets its first glimpse of the outside world and its parents.

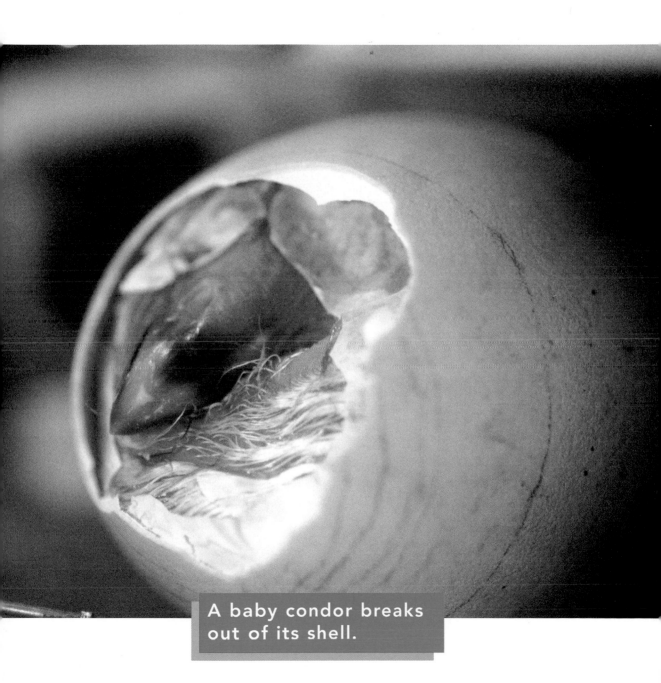

A baby condor breaks out of its shell.

A baby condor must learn to fly and find food.

The parents have worked hard to incubate their egg, but their work is far from done. They must feed the baby condor often. Then they must teach it to fly and to find its own food. The young condor won't leave its parents until it is more than a year old.

Scientists Hatch a Plan

In 1930, scientists counted about two hundred condors in North America. Fifty years later, fewer than twenty-five wild condors remained.

What was happening to the condors? Many people worried that the bird would

Few condors were found in the wild in the 1970s.

soon disappear altogether. They didn't want the condors to become **extinct**. A group of scientists got together to study the problem and came up with a plan.

The plan had two parts. Scientists hoped to start a group of **captive** birds with wild condor eggs. The scientists would also capture wild condors and mate them. Once the birds laid eggs, scientists would hatch them in a special

A scientist helps a condor break out of its egg.

laboratory. Scientists would then raise and train the young birds. Finally, they would release the birds into the wild.

Not everyone thought the plan would work. What if the birds wouldn't mate? Would they survive being caught and kept in a cage? No one had even hatched a condor egg outside of the nest.

Yet, why were the condors disappearing? No one knew for sure, but they soon discovered

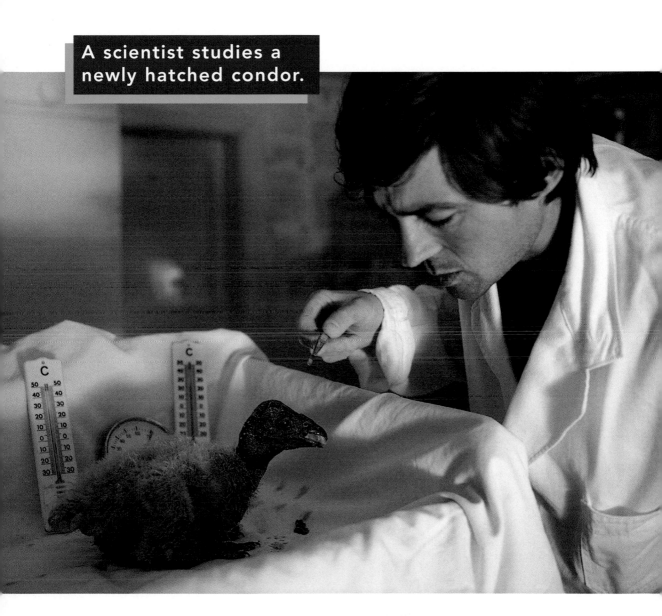

A scientist studies a newly hatched condor.

Researchers attach a transmitter to a condor so they can track it in the wild.

one possible answer. One day scientists found a dead condor in the wild. Studies of the body showed high levels of lead—a poison. The lead came from the pellets of a shotgun. Although the condor hadn't been shot, it had fed on an animal that had been. Condors were dying for other reasons too. Some condors, for example, ran into power lines, while others were shot by ranchers or hunters.

Condor Comeback

Today about fifty condors fly free. In addition, more than one hundred condors live in three breeding centers. These centers still breed captive condors and release them into the wild. The rescue plan seems to be working!

These condors
live at a special
breeding center.

But questions still remain. Many of the released birds are not grown up. Will they select mates when the time comes? Will the pairs be able to raise young condors? Can they teach them what they need to know to survive? We can only wait and hope.

It is too soon to tell what will happen to condors released from captivity.

To Find Out More

If you'd like to learn more about the California condor, check out these additional resources.

Books

Arnold, Caroline. **On the Brink of Extinction: The California Condor.** Harcourt Brace Jovanovich Publishers, 1993.

Peters, Lisa. **The Condor.** Crestwood House, 1990.

Schorsch, Nancy. **Saving the Condor.** Franklin Watts, 1991.

Silverstein, Alvin. Virginia Silverstein, and Laura Silverstein Nunn. **The California Condor.** Millbrook Press, 1998.

☼ Organizations and Online Sites

**American Zoo and
Aquarium Association**
8403 Colesville Road,
Suite 710
Silver Spring, MD
20910-3314
*http://aza.org/Programs/
SSP/ssp.cfm?ssp=18*

Los Angeles Zoo
5333 Zoo Drive
Los Angeles, CA 90027
*http://www.lazoo.org/
cfacts.htm*

National Audubon Society
950 Third Avenue
New York, NY 10022
http://www.audubon.org

The Peregrine Fund
566 W. Flying Hawk Lane
Boise, ID 83709
*http://www.peregrinefund.
org/notes_condor.html*

**San Diego Wild
Animal Park**
15500 San Pasqual Valley
Road
Escondido, CA 92027
*http://www.sandiegozoo.
org/cres/milestone.html*

**United States Fish &
Wildlife Service**
U.S. Department
of the Interior
Hopper Mountain
NWR Complex
California Condor
Recovery Program
P.O. Box 5839
Ventura, CA 93005
*http://www.r1.fws.gov/
news/9923.htm*

*http://species.fws.gov/
bio_cond.html*

Important Words

captive a person or other animal caught and held as a prisoner

endangered species a kind of living thing that is in danger of dying out

extinct no longer living. Usually refers to a type of living thing that once lived on Earth but has died out.

incubate to protect and keep warm in order to allow for growth and development

predator an animal that hunts other animals for food

scavenger an animal that feeds on dead animals and rotting meat

thermal a type of air current that is formed near the ground and then rises. The current is created as the cool air near the surface heats up and lifts upward.

vulture a type of bird that feeds mostly on dead animals, has a bare head with no feathers, and blunt, weak claws

Index

Meet the Author

Patricia A. Fink Martin holds a doctorate in biology. After spending many years teaching and working in the laboratory, she began writing science books for children. In 1998, *Booklist* chose her first book, *Animals that Walk on Water*, as one of the ten best animal books for children for that year. She has since published eight more books. Dr. Martin lives in Tennessee with her husband Jerry, their daughter Leslie, and their golden retriever Ginger.

Photographs © 2002: Animals Animals/Mark A. Chappell: 2; Corbis Images: 17, 42 (AFP), 23 (W. Perry Conway); Joel Sartore: 9 bottom, 20, 21, 25, 35, 41; Peter Arnold Inc.: 37 (Y. Arthus-Bertrand), cover, 7, 15, 19, 43 (Ted Schiffman); Photo Researchers, NY: 1 (Jeff Apoian), 4 (Jerry L. Ferrara), 11, 13, 16, 33 (Tom McHugh), 9 top (Anthony Mercieca); Visuals Unlimited/Wm. Grenfell: 38; Zoological Society of San Diego: 27, 29, 30.